— *The* —
SINNER / SAINT
LENTEN DEVOTIONAL

BY: KYLE G. JONES AND
KATHRYN STRAUCH

Foreword by:
DANIEL EMERY PRICE

The Sinner/Saint Lenten Devotional

Published by:
1517 Publishing
PO Box 54032
Irvine, CA 92619-4032

Publisher's Cataloging-In-Publication Data
(Prepared by The Donohue Group, Inc.)

Names: Jones, Kyle G., author. | Strauch, Kathryn, author. | Price, Daniel
            Emery, writer of supplementary textual content.
Title: The sinner/saint Lenten devotional / by Kyle G. Jones and Kathryn
            Strauch ; foreword by Daniel Emery Price.
Other Titles: Sinner saint Lenten devotional
Description: Irvine, CA : 1517 Publishing, [2019] | Includes
            bibliographical references and index.
Identifiers: ISBN 9781948969130 (softcover) | ISBN 9781948969147 (ebook)
Subjects: LCSH: Lent--Prayers and devotions. | Lutheran Church--Prayers
            and devotions. | Bible--Meditations. | Devotional exercises.
Classification: LCC BX8067.L5 J66 2019 (print) | LCC BX8067.L5 (ebook) |
            DDC 242/.34--dc23

Printed in the United States of America

Cover art by Brenton Clarke Little.

—— *The* ——
SINNER / SAINT
LENTEN DEVOTIONAL

Contents

THIRD WEEK OF LENT

FOURTH WEEK OF LENT

FIFTH WEEK OF LENT

HOLY WEEK

Foreword

PROPERLY SPEAKING, REPENTANCE CONSISTS OF TWO
PARTS: ONE PART IS CONTRITION, OR THE TERRORS THAT
STRIKE THE CONSCIENCE THROUGH KNOWLEDGE OF
SIN. THE OTHER PART IS FAITH, WHICH IS BORN OF THE
GOSPEL, OR THE ABSOLUTION, AND BELIEVES THAT FOR
CHRIST'S SAKE, SINS ARE FORGIVEN.

The Augsburg Confession, 1530

I once saw a man holding a sign that read:

Divorce is an abomination. Repent!

That's it. Nothing else. Nothing about forgiveness. Nothing about God. Nothing about Christ or His blood-soaked cross and empty tomb. I couldn't help but approach the man and ask him one question.

"Repent to what?"

He didn't answer. In fact, he wouldn't even look at me. I asked the question again...still nothing. So I told him about all that Christ had done for a world of wretched sinners, and I asked him to consider adding some good news to his sign if he was dead set on holding one. Sadly, he never spoke to me. Never even looked at me. But he certainly heard me.

"Repentance" is a word we use a lot in Christianity. All of the Old Testament Prophets said to repent. John the Baptist said to repent. Jesus said to repent. The Apostles said to repent. Repentance is a big deal. Understandably, we feel the pressure to get this right—but far too often we get it wrong.

Because the Church is made up of sinners, we don't have to look far to find a Christian who has blown it in every possible way—and if we're going to go looking, we should look in the mirror. The Bible tells us plainly: "*no one does good, not even one*" and "*if we claim to be without sin, we deceive ourselves and the truth is not in us.*" (Romans 3:12 & 1 John 1:8)

So we repent. But if repentance is such a big deal, how do we know when someone is truly repentant? What signs do they show? What language do they use? And who decides?

We tend to put a person's repentance under the microscope to determine if it is genuine or not. Are they really sorry? Let's take a look. Have they wept enough, felt ashamed enough, did they use the word "sin" enough, and so on. It all goes under the microscope. And this microscope is usually found in the hypocritical Laboratory of Public Opinion, where all manner of religious mad science takes place.

In Luke 15, Jesus tells us a parable about a Father and his two sons. It is here where we see what repentance looks like and how grace responds to it. Just like the definition above from *The Augsburg Confession*, "repentance consists of two parts." Contrition is the Prodigal's return, and Absolution is the Father's response.

We all know the story. The younger son leaves home and blows his inheritance on self-centered hedonism. He finally comes to the end of himself while feeding pigs and being tempted to join them for dinner. The Law does its work. The son knows he has sinned. He knows there is no excuse for what he has done. But maybe, just maybe, his good Father will take him in as a servant. Perhaps he can prove just how sorry he is. Perhaps he can work off his sins. So the Prodigal heads home, practicing his confession and request with every step back.

When the Father sees his wayward son coming down the road, he doesn't look through any binoculars. There is no checking to see if his shoulders are slumped enough, if his head is hung low enough, or if his cheeks are tear-streaked enough. Instead, the Father flings open the doors and runs out to embrace his son.

The Prodigal only had it half right. Repentance doesn't look like cutting a deal with your Father to work off your sins, but it does look like going home.

> **Grace doesn't investigate a homebound son. Grace runs out to embrace him with love. It doesn't scream, "Bring me the microscope!" It says, "Bring the best robe and shoes. Give him a ring and fire up the barbecue—because we're about to celebrate!"**

Grace doesn't respond to repentance by asking, "Why couldn't you be more like your older brother?" Or... "Will you promise never to do this again?" Grace never says, "I told you so." Grace doesn't listen to a word of your well thought out work plan for redemption." Grace interrupts you with words of mercy so outrageous they make your own brother object. Grace gives each Prodigal every reason to believe the good news that he is forgiven. All is as it was before—"*It is finished.*"

What is repentance? It's nothing to be investigated. Nothing to be dissected.

It's a gift to be celebrated. Put away the microscopes and fling open the doors, because *"It is fitting to celebrate and be glad, your brother was dead, and is alive; he was lost, and is found."* (Luke 15:32) Repentance is going home where all is forgiven.

In this beautiful devotional volume, Kathy and Kyle explore this wonderful gift called repentance and turn the reader back to Christ and His finished work on every page. There is no repentance apart from Christ. There is no Lent apart from His suffering on our behalf. There is no hope apart from His righteousness gifted to us. The authors know all of these things. Dear Sinner/Saint, prepare to told to go home to your forgiving Father over and over.

- DANIEL EMERY PRICE

ASH WEDNESDAY

Marked

DO YOU NOT KNOW THAT ALL OF US WHO
HAVE BEEN BAPTIZED INTO CHRIST JESUS
WERE BAPTIZED INTO HIS DEATH?

Romans 6:3

On Ash Wednesday, sinners and saints leave church marked with a cross, marked with the sign and material of death. Heads become canvases painted with ashes. The sobering words, "for you are dust, and to dust you shall return" (Genesis 3:19) spoken to Adam and Eve as they rebelled against the Lord, are echoed today.

The season of Lent is a time of repentance. We, like our first parents, have rebelled against the Lord, not once, not twice, but countless times. We are sinners, transgressors, rebels of our Creator; we too have become poisoned with death and marked by our transgressions.

Repentance never ends with the Law. Repentance does not conclude with confession. God-given repentance always finds its consummation in Christ. In the Augsburg Confession, the Reformers spoke of repentance in this way:

After his sin Adam is reproved and becomes terrified; this was contrition. Afterward God promises grace, and speaks of a future seed (the blessed seed, i.e., Christ), by which the kingdom of the devil, death, and sin will be destroyed; there he offers the remission of sins. These are the chief things.

Today, heads become canvases painted with ashes. Yet, it is not our death imposed on our heads but Jesus's death for us. Jesus became the dust that we are, for us.

> **Our sin marked Christ. Jesus was marked with the scars of nails and a spear for us. His hands, feet, and side are marked with scars displaying the cost of our redemption.**

We are no longer marked by our sin but by our Savior. We have a watery seal placed upon us by our Lord, who marks us as his own in baptism through water and the word. The marks of dust and ashes on the heads of worshipers today point beyond our death—they direct our eyes of faith to the death of our substitute, who was marked for us.

Heavenly Father, bring us to a daily remembrance of our baptisms so we may die to our sinful nature and look to you alone for forgiveness, life, and salvation.

Amen.

FOR FURTHER REFLECTION, READ ROMANS 6:3–11

Meeting Jesus in the Water

IN THE FOURTH WATCH OF THE NIGHT [JESUS] CAME TO THEM, WALKING ON THE SEA. BUT WHEN THE DISCIPLES SAW HIM WALKING ON THE SEA, THEY WERE TERRIFIED, AND SAID, "IT IS A GHOST!" AND THEY CRIED OUT IN FEAR. BUT IMMEDIATELY JESUS SPOKE TO THEM, SAYING, "TAKE HEART; IT IS I. DO NOT BE AFRAID."

Matthew 14:25-27

Wind whipped water into fear-filled eyes. Waves crashed as the sea had its way with the boat. The vessel became as weighted with water as their minds became burdened with terror.

After a turbulent night at sea, the disciples finally saw Jesus. But instead of finding comfort, their fear intensified.

Immediately Jesus spoke to them. He did not hesitate to calm their terror-stricken cries. In three short words, Jesus calmed their fear. Three simple words, "It is I," recalled their fleeting faith.

The one who spoke through the wind and waves that stormy night is the same one who speaks to us. Christ says to us, "Take heart; it is I. Do not be afraid." The feet that stood and walked on water are the same feet that were nailed to a cross for you. The one who walked on water walked up to Jerusalem for you.

> **Take heart. It is Jesus. It is Jesus who comes to us, not on the waves of the sea but in the waters of baptism. Do not be afraid—the Jesus who stood on the water now stands on the head of the serpent.**

Heavenly Father, when the waves of worry and guilt threaten to overtake us, be with us always as you have promised when you claimed us as your own when you came to us in the waters of our baptism. Amen.

FOR FURTHER REFLECTION, READ 1 PETER 3:18–22.

The Watery Grave

THEN JESUS CAME FROM GALILEE TO THE JORDAN TO JOHN, TO BE BAPTIZED BY HIM. JOHN WOULD HAVE PREVENTED HIM, SAYING, "I NEED TO BE BAPTIZED BY YOU, AND DO YOU COME TO ME?" BUT JESUS ANSWERED HIM, "LET IT BE SO NOW, FOR THUS IT IS FITTING FOR US TO FULFILL ALL RIGHTEOUSNESS."

Matthew 3:13-15

The calm ripples of the river stirred as sinners stepped into its water. Innumerable sinners polluted these waters in the wilderness. The banks of the Jordan acted as a sponge, absorbing the confessions of the penitent. It became a graveyard filled with biographies of sinners.

Day after day John stood on the banks of the Jordan River preaching repentance and forgiveness, Law, and Gospel. As John called sinners to repentance, the one about whom John prophesied stood on its banks. The Lord had come himself to receive John's baptism of repentance.

What was Jesus doing? Jesus was the one, the only one, who did not need a baptism of repentance. He committed no sin. He always feared, loved, and trusted in God above all things. He always, without fail, loved his neighbor as himself. There was no fault in him. Why would Jesus come?

> **For us Jesus was baptized. For us Jesus received a baptism of repentance. For us Jesus absorbed all the sin of the sinners who stepped into the banks of the river. In his baptism, Jesus stood in the place of sinners and united himself with us. Jesus insisted that he be united to us in those waters.**

Our baptismal font becomes a sunken tomb. "In a wat'ry grave are buried All our sins that Jesus carried,"[1] writes hymnist Stephen Starke. In the waters of Jesus baptism, he received our sin. In our baptism, we receive Jesus's righteousness. On the banks of the Jordan, Jesus began his journey to the cross.

Heavenly Father, you sent your Son, who united himself to us in the waters of baptism. He took our sins upon himself and gave us his righteousness. Bring us to daily repentance and remembrance of our baptism as you daily forgive and keep us in the faith. Amen.

> **FOR FURTHER REFLECTION, READ MATTHEW 3:11–17.**

---

[1] Starke, Stephen P. Lutheran Service Book. Pew Edition ed. Saint Louis, MO: Concordia Publishing House, 2006. 597

The Master Artist

"IF YOU ARE THE SON OF GOD..."

Matthew 4:3

Crafty. Of all the words at his disposal, Moses chose to describe the serpent in Genesis as crafty. The apostle Peter later portrayed the devil as a prowling lion. One thing from scripture is certain: we have an enemy skulking around us, patiently lurking in the shadows of uncertainty, waiting for the opportune time to assault our faith.

At Jesus's baptism the Father said, "This is my beloved Son, with whom I am well pleased" (Matthew 3:17). Then, driven into the wilderness, hungry and weakened by the harsh desert wasteland, Jesus was met by our adversary.

The devil began his attack with one word: if. With two little letters, he floods our imaginations with questions of doubt so he can drown our faith. When the devil prowls around our Lord, his weaponry consists of one word meant to thwart the word of God: if. "If you are the Son of God ..." (Matthew 4:3).

Martin Luther once wrote that the devil is the master of a thousand arts. Satan paints a masterpiece of exquisite lies on the canvas in our minds. He sketches a portrait of our heavenly Father that is deceitful and unloving. These little seeds of doubt have the potential to grow weeds of disbelief in the word of God. The language of the devil seeks to make demands of God's promises rather than receiving them as gifts in faith.

> **Luther continued, "What, then, shall we call God's Word, which routs and destroys this master of a thousand arts with all his wiles and might? It must, indeed, be master of more than a hundred thousand arts."[2]**

Instead of gazing at the masterpiece of lies our foe has woven together, Jesus drove away temptation with the word of God. Jesus endured the harassment and vexation of the tempter, withstanding temptation in our place.

Heavenly Father, when we fall prey to the tempter's powers, hold us fast with your word, and remind us of what you have done for us. Gift us with faith so that we may boldly trust your promises. Amen.

FOR FURTHER REFLECTION, READ GENESIS 3:1–15.

---

[2] Tappert, Theodore G. The Book of Concord: The Confessions of the Evangelical Lutheran Church. Philadelphia, PA: Fortress Press, 1959. 360

FIRST WEEK *of* LENT

The God Who Sees

SO SHE CALLED THE NAME OF THE LORD WHO SPOKE TO HER, "YOU ARE A GOD OF SEEING," FOR SHE SAID, "TRULY HERE I HAVE SEEN HIM WHO LOOKS AFTER ME."

Genesis 16:13

The scorching heat and sand of the desert wasteland became more bearable than staying with Sarai, her mistress. As Hagar found respite in a spring of water, the Lord found her. And he talked with her. An afflicted and distressed runaway servant sat in the wilderness conversing with God.

After their exchange, Hagar overflowed with praise to the God, whom she had now seen. In her exaltation, she did not choose to acclaim him as the God who is merciful, faithful, just, or compassionate—though she could have. Hagar chose the verb seeing to extol God. He is the God who sees.

The Lord has seen us in our affliction by sin, death, and the devil. He has seen and does not turn his face away from us but rather turns it toward us in Christ.

The Lord Hagar named is the Lord who names us, who places his name upon us. Norman Nagel expresses the significance of this when he writes, "When the Lord puts his name on something, he marks it as his own ... Where his name is located, he is committed by that name to see to its good."[3]

The Lord is the God who sees us, who baptized us and made us his own. He is the God who forgives, blesses, and sanctifies. He is the God who sees sinners and does not turn away. The Lord is the God who sees and provides, who feeds his children at his table so he might wash away their sins and draw them to himself again and again.

Heavenly Father, you will always look upon us in favor because of your love and sacrifice for us. Grant us eyes of faith to see you for the good and gracious God you are and will always be for us. Amen.

FOR FURTHER REFLECTION, READ NUMBERS 6:22–27.

[3] Nagel, Norman E. Lutheran Worship History and Practice. Saint Louis, MO: Concordia Publishing House, 1993. 263-264

Divine Servant

JESUS, KNOWING THAT THE FATHER HAD
GIVEN ALL THINGS INTO HIS HANDS, AND
THAT HE HAD COME FROM GOD AND WAS
GOING BACK TO GOD, ROSE FROM SUPPER.
HE LAID ASIDE HIS OUTER GARMENTS, AND
TAKING A TOWEL, TIED IT AROUND HIS WAIST.
THEN HE POURED WATER INTO A BASIN AND
BEGAN TO WASH THE DISCIPLES' FEET AND
TO WIPE THEM WITH THE TOWEL THAT WAS
WRAPPED AROUND HIM.

John 13:3–5

Jesus had authority over everything. The apostle John tells us that all things were delivered into Jesus's hands.

Now, knowing this, how does Jesus use his authority?

> *He laid aside his outer garments, and taking a towel, tied it around his waist. Then, he poured water into a basin and began to wash the disciples' feet and to wipe them with the towel that was wrapped around him. (John 13:4-5)*

Jesus uses his divine authority and power to serve sinners.

The King of kings and Lord of lords, the Alpha and the Omega, when given the universe, knelt before sinners to wash their grimy, smelly feet. Jesus does not stand far off or high above. Instead he bends down, placing himself in the position of the lowliest servant. This is our God.

The hands that were given all power and authority reached out to take the dirty feet of sinners. The righteous one who has the authority to condemn sinners takes our sin and gives us his righteousness.

The Divine Servant uses his reign to save sinners. His kingdom comes and his will is done as sinners are continually bathed by God himself in the basin of the baptismal font. The Divine Servant continually bends down to wash dirty souls. He cleanses them with water and the word. We are baptized, made clean, and washed in the righteousness of Christ.

Heavenly Father, you have washed us in the waters of our baptism. As we walk with you toward the cross this Lent, may we treasure the gifts you continually give to us which were won for us at Calvary. Amen.

FOR FURTHER REFLECTION, READ JOHN 13:1–20.

Dying of Thirst

BLESSED ARE THOSE WHO HUNGER AND
THIRST FOR RIGHTEOUSNESS, FOR THEY
SHALL BE SATISFIED.

Matthew 5:6

His tongue stuck to the roof of his mouth. Exhausted and dehydrated from the journey, the stranger found a well where he could rest his weary feet. As he found respite from the journey, a woman drew near.

This woman had not come to welcome this visitor as he passed through. She came in shame. While most sought shelter in the sweltering heat, shuffling feet kicked up sand and dirt as they scurried to gather water under the shelter of the scorching sun. However, to the weary traveler, this was not just another woman. He engaged her in a conversation. He knew her. She was the reason he had to go through this town. He saw her before she ever knew him, and he loved her. She was his beloved despite the sin and shame that drove her here in the first place.

She was dying of thirst. It ran deeper than the well water could satisfy. She was dehydrated by her sin and thirsty for righteousness. The one who sat before her speaking to her was himself the fountain of living water that alone could satisfy. He was her righteousness.

> **This living water had come to be thirsty for her. The one who met her at the well would later cry out, "I thirst," as he drank dry her cup of sin and shame. Water and blood would stream from the side of her God as he gave his life for her guilt and was pierced for her.**

We too have been met by Jesus at a well. We have been greeted by our Lord, who knows us completely, who knew us before we were even born. Our past, present, and future are laid bare before him. He knows our sin and shame. He knows everything about us, yet he still loves us with an everlasting love. At the well of the baptismal font, Jesus pours out his living water upon us. He quenches our thirsty souls with himself.

Heavenly Father, you know everything we've ever done. Yet, you will not leave us in our shame. Fill us with your righteousness and remind us of our baptism, when you came to us and filled us with your living water. Amen.

FOR FURTHER REFLECTION, READ JOHN 4:1–45.

A Tale of Two Prayers

OH GIVE THANKS TO THE LORD, FOR HE IS GOOD;
FOR HIS STEADFAST LOVE ENDURES FOREVER!
...LET THOSE WHO FEAR THE LORD SAY, "HIS
STEADFAST LOVE ENDURES FOREVER."

Psalm 118:1, 4

The sweet smell of incense rose from the temple as he walked through the gates. The Pharisee had come to offer prayers of thanksgiving. He had so much to be thankful for, after all.

He had it all: health, wealth, and prosperity. Surely this was a divine confirmation of God's favor on his life. After all, he was not like other men, extortioners, unjust, adulterers, or even that tax collector crouching in the shadows of the temple. His obedience to every facet of the law was impeccable. In fact, he went above and beyond. This man fasted twice a week and gave tithes of all he received. He was the gold standard for moral living.

The pharisee's prayer was a prayer of thanksgiving. "O give thanks to the Lord, for I am good. My obedience endures forever!"

Cowering in the shadows of the temple was a figure too ashamed to step into the light and be seen. He too had a life full of health, wealth, and prosperity. However, this man did not thank God for his successful life but begged God to have mercy on him.

Indeed, God had mercy on him; the tax collector went home justified. The two temple guests offered prayers of thanksgiving, but only one was able to pour out a truly thankful heart to the Lord.

From the forgiveness the tax collector received swelled a prayer of thanksgiving.

> **O give thanks to the LORD for he is good; for his steadfast love endures forever! ... Let those who fear the LORD say "His steadfast love endures forever." Out of my distress I called on the LORD; the LORD answered me and set me free. (Psalm 118:1, 4–5)**

The Lord's goodness is this: his steadfast love endures forever. He alone is good and pours out his good gospel gifts without end. His steadfast love remains for sinners forever. His steadfast love remains and covers over the iniquities of those who are least deserving, the ungodly, the tax collector, the pharisee, *and us.*

Heavenly Father, forgive us for the times we pray as the pharisee, looking to our own works instead of the works you have done for us. Give us faith to trust your promise and thankful hearts for your faithful love toward us. Amen.

FOR FURTHER REFLECTION, READ LUKE 18:9–14.

Delivered into Evil?

PRAY THEN LIKE THIS: "OUR FATHER IN HEAVEN, HALLOWED BE YOUR NAME. YOUR KINGDOM COME, YOUR WILL BE DONE, ON EARTH AS IT IS IN HEAVEN. GIVE US THIS DAY OUR DAILY BREAD, AND FORGIVE US OUR DEBTS, AS WE ALSO HAVE FORGIVEN OUR DEBTORS. AND LEAD US NOT INTO TEMPTATION, BUT DELIVER US FROM EVIL."

Matthew 6:9–13

We do not know how to pray. It gets worse. Left to ourselves, we do not seek God (Romans 3:11). We do not run to our heavenly Father. We do not call on him in every trouble, praying, praising, and giving thanks.

That was the bad news. The good news—Jesus teaches us to pray. The Lord himself gives to us the words and petitions we are to bring to our heavenly Father. Our brother, Christ, prays with us and for us. He guides us into the arms of our loving heavenly Father.

In the prayer our Lord gave us, Jesus teaches us to pray, "deliver us from evil." He promises to hear our prayer and answer the prayer he himself taught us to pray. Our Lord's promises are not empty words. When our God makes a promise, he is faithful to carry out that promise. He carries out his promises even to his own death for us.

The very one who gave us these words, "deliver us from evil," is the one who was delivered into the consequences of our evil deeds. He was handed over to the desires of wicked men. Jesus was delivered into the hands of sin, death, and the power of the devil for us. Our deliverer died the death and experienced the hell our evil deeds merited. On the third day he rose, breaking the jaws of our captors and delivering us into his gracious hands.

> **In the Lutheran liturgy we begin the prayer with this preface: "trusting his promises we are bold to pray." Trusting in Jesus's promises, we are bold to come before our heavenly Father, knowing he will meet our every need.**

Martin Luther sums up this petition in a hymn, "from evil, Lord, deliver us; the times and days are perilous. Redeem us from eternal death, And, when we yield our dying breath, Console us, grant us calm release, And take our souls to You in peace." Our Lord has delivered us through his death and resurrection and continually grants us this peace as he comforts us through word and sacrament.

Heavenly Father, you have delivered us from evil. Grant us faith to come to you in boldness to approach you with every need and thanksgiving. Amen.

FOR FURTHER REFLECTION, READ PSALM 116.

Jesus's Devotion

AFTER THIS MANY OF HIS DISCIPLES TURNED
BACK AND NO LONGER WALKED WITH HIM. SO
JESUS SAID TO THE TWELVE, "DO YOU WANT TO
GO AWAY AS WELL?" SIMON PETER ANSWERED
HIM, "LORD, TO WHOM SHALL WE GO? YOU HAVE
THE WORDS OF ETERNAL LIFE, AND WE HAVE
BELIEVED, AND HAVE COME TO KNOW, THAT
YOU ARE THE HOLY ONE OF GOD."

John 6:66–69

Just like that, the crowd dissipated. Jesus's words pierced like a bright light through their foggy misconceptions. The hungry mouths that touched, chewed, and swallowed a miracle now grumbled in discontent. Tired feet that traversed around the lake were leaving a cloud of dust behind them as they left.

Briefly glance at John 6, and you will see a chapter bursting with miracles and masses encircling Jesus. Jesus fed over five thousand, walked on water, and spoke, and then his following plummeted. His sermon initiated an exodus.

Jesus turned to his closest disciples and asked the disheartening question, "Do you want to go away as well?" Peter, true to his character, immediately shattered the silence. "Lord, to whom shall we go? You have the words of eternal life."

Peter was devoted to Jesus. He was a man who was ready in a heartbeat to demonstrate devotion for his Lord. There was such certainty in Peter that he trusted his Jesus would uphold him on the water rather than letting the sea swallow him alive. He would stake his life on that fact. However, that was not how Peter responded to Jesus's question here.

Peter's response did not insinuate his tenacious, often-vocal, faith. He attributed Jesus's words as the reason for remaining. Martin Luther writes, "So completely does everything depend on God's mercy that even the apostles cannot be trusted. Not a single one of them can say: 'I am so strong. I do not fear that I will fall.' The indispensable requisite is God's blessing, or these words: 'I chose you.'"[4]

We are fickle and faithless. Our relationship with Christ is not initiated by or contingent on our faithfulness. The center of faith is not anchored in our ability to demonstrate our devotion to Christ. The center of faith is **Christ** and **his work for us**. Faith embraces Christ, who remained devoted unto death for us.

Heavenly Father, to whom shall we go? You give to us the word of everlasting life. As you have chosen us, keep us in your grace until life everlasting. Amen.

> **FOR FURTHER REFLECTION, READ EPHESIANS 1:1–14.**

---

[4] Luther, Martin. Sermons on the Gospel of St. John Chapters 6-8. American Edition ed. Vol. 23. Luther's Works. Saint Louis, MO: Concordia Publishing House, 1959. 190

Buried Treasure

THE KINGDOM OF HEAVEN IS LIKE TREASURE HIDDEN IN A FIELD, WHICH A MAN FOUND AND COVERED UP. THEN IN HIS JOY HE GOES AND SELLS ALL THAT HE HAS AND BUYS THAT FIELD.

Matthew 13:44

It's Lent. So, what have you given up for Jesus? How much is Jesus really worth to you? Would you forsake everything for him? If Jesus were to ask you to sell everything and come follow him, would you? Upon finding Jesus, like a treasure hidden in a field, would you sell everything you own just to have him?

So often we take parables, such as this parable of the treasure hidden in a field, and find ourselves front and center running the verbs. We understand this parable to be first and foremost about what we must do for God. Our old Adam goes to work searching scripture for a step-by-step instructional guide on how to gain his salvation. However, this parable, like all parables, is not about us; it's about what Jesus does for *us*.

We do not go out in joy and sell all that we have for God. We cannot. We are, as the scriptures state, dead in our trespasses and sin. We are bankrupt. We have nothing to give to God except our debt of sin.

Lent is about good news, gospel joy. In short, *Lent is about Jesus for you. Lent is about Jesus who, finding a treasure hidden in a field, for joy over it goes and sells all that he has to purchase it.* Or as the writer to the Hebrews states, "[Jesus] for the joy that was set before him endured the cross, despising the shame, and is seated at the right hand of the throne of God" (Hebrews 12:2).

> **We have been bought, redeemed, purchased, not with earthly wealth but with Jesus himself. Jesus, for joy over us, gave up his life so he may call us his own. For joy Jesus spilled his blood to redeem us.**

Heavenly Father, you have given your Son up for our sins. With his own holy blood, you purchased us and call us your treasure. During this season of Lent, may we ponder and rejoice in your sacrifice for us that made us your own. Amen.

FOR FURTHER REFLECTION, READ PSALM 32.

SECOND WEEK *of* LENT

Jesus Doesn't Give out Clean Slates

FOR I AM NOT ASHAMED OF THE GOSPEL,
FOR IT IS THE POWER OF GOD FOR SALVATION
TO EVERYONE WHO BELIEVES, TO THE JEW
FIRST AND ALSO TO THE GREEK. FOR IN IT
THE RIGHTEOUSNESS OF GOD IS REVEALED
FROM FAITH FOR FAITH, AS IT IS WRITTEN,
"THE RIGHTEOUS SHALL LIVE BY FAITH."

Romans 1:16-17

Christians employ the *clean slate* analogy to illustrate the comfort of God's forgiveness in the Christian's daily life. But this analogy can lead the comforted soul to a new place of terror. This return to a terrified conscience comes from a weakness in the clean slate analogy. It shows only part of Christ's work.

The part of Christ's work it shows is true and good news. We rack up an incalculable number of sins in a single day. A four-by-eight-foot classroom whiteboard couldn't contain them, let alone a personal-sized writing slate. To have our mess before

God erased by God himself on the cross brings unspeakable joy!

But the clean slate analogy throws us back onto the Law of God. It fails to recognize the sinful nature that still lives within us. The analogy assumes we have the power within us to fill the slate God has cleaned with good works. But we can't. We begin to believe that the status of our standing before God depends on what we fill the clean slate with. Whatever comfort the clean slate provided vanishes when our sins cover our slate again.

Jesus's death does earn forgiveness, which he daily and freely gives to us. He does take our sin-filled slate and wipe it clean. But Jesus doesn't hand it back blank. Instead, he hands it back written on. What's written on it? The righteousness of God.

We cling to the truth of the cross: Jesus earned *for us* and gives *to us* forgiveness, salvation, and life by his death and resurrection. But Jesus gives us even more. Christ also imputes to us his righteousness: his perfect life and his obedience to the will of the Father. This he gives along with forgiveness and life.

Jesus doesn't give out clean slates. He cleans them of our sin, to be sure. But before he hands them back, he fills them with his righteousness. This is God's gospel economy in action. As Paul teaches in 2 Corinthians 5:21, "For our sake [God] made him to be sin who knew no sin, so that in him we might become the righteousness of God."

Heavenly Father, thank you for cleaning our slate and handing it back filled with your Son's righteousness. Amen.

FOR FURTHER REFLECTION, READ ROMANS 1:1–17.

The Great Hide and Seek

AND THEY HEARD THE SOUND OF THE LORD
GOD WALKING IN THE GARDEN IN THE COOL
OF THE DAY, AND THE MAN AND HIS WIFE HID
THEMSELVES FROM THE PRESENCE OF THE LORD
GOD AMONG THE TREES OF THE GARDEN. BUT
THE LORD GOD CALLED TO THE MAN AND
SAID TO HIM, "WHERE ARE YOU?"

Genesis 3:8-9

You've just made the biggest mistake of your life. Regret rushes down upon you like an avalanche. Suddenly, you're not alone. Someone's coming. Your eyes widen. You realize you need to hide.

From your concealment, the sounds of their movement grows louder, closer. Your terror grows. *Please don't find me, please don't find me, please don't find me*. Then the movement stops. The seeker stands still. You hear a voice, calm and even. "Where are you?"

God's first words, in response to the first sin, come as a question. He knows where Adam and Eve hid themselves. He knows what they did. Yet, as all-knowing and all-powerful, he didn't come to destroy them in fire and fury. He came to them and called to them.

God comes and calls to us in the same way. We confess our sin because God has called to us: "Where are you?" We stand exposed before him. He knows full well why we hid and what we did. But he still asks, "Did you do what I told you not to?" He listens to our excuses, our blame-shifting, our self-justifying reasons. Still he asks, "What is this you have done?" Finally, the truth is laid bare. "My self-righteousness deceived me, and I did what you told me not to."

> **But God doesn't leave us to our sin and misery. He forgives. Jesus's words evidence this. He "came to seek and to save the lost" (Luke 19:10). He "came not to call the righteous, but sinners" (Matthew 9:13). He came to save us sinners from our sin (Matthew 1:21). He came "that [we] may have life and have it abundantly" (John 10:10).**

God calls us out from behind our fig leaves of self-righteousness and the bushes of works we use to conceal ourselves. He calls to us, not to destroy us but to restore us. He calls to us to show us his mercy, to give us his grace, to announce that in Christ Jesus, our sins are forgiven. As he spoke the first gospel promise, the *protoevangelium*, to Adam and Eve (Genesis 3:15), he speaks to us the same gospel, now fulfilled through his word made flesh: "My Son has fulfilled the promises. You are forgiven by his work. He took your sin and gives you his righteousness. You, who once hid yourself, are now found forgiven in me."

Heavenly Father, thank you for sending your Son to fulfill the promise of salvation you made to our first parents, the first sinners, that we may have life. Amen.

FOR FURTHER REFLECTION, READ GENESIS 3:1–15.

For Our Benefit

HAVE THIS MIND AMONG YOURSELVES, WHICH IS YOURS IN CHRIST JESUS, WHO, THOUGH HE WAS IN THE FORM OF GOD, DID NOT COUNT EQUALITY WITH GOD A THING TO BE GRASPED.

Philippians 2:5-6

We're always on the lookout for an advantage over others—something that gives us an edge over the competition (a.k.a., our neighbors). If we had an inkling of the power Jesus possessed as both divine and human, we would certainly use it to benefit ourselves over our neighbors. But Jesus, though he was both fully divine and fully human, didn't.

Jesus had every opportunity to use his divinity to his advantage. He could have come to earth in riches and wealth. He could have arranged it so he could hobnob and schmooze with the elite, out of sight of the poor and oppressed. He could have amassed a large earthly army, combined it with an army of angels, and swept over the world, conquering everyone and everything. But he didn't.

Even during his ministry, Jesus refrained from using his divinity for his own benefit. He could have instilled his disciples with a wisdom that gave them perfect understanding of his will and desire. He could have controlled them to perfectly carry out his commands. He could have avoided touching lepers to heal them, eating with tax collectors to teach them, and associating with women of ill repute to redeem them. But he didn't.

Instead of using his divinity for his own advantage and benefit, the Son of God used it for ours. He could have given up on humanity the moment we messed up his perfect creation. Instead, he made a promise to fix it. And he kept that promise. He gave up his advantage as God on high to become God made man. He gave up his advantage to dwell in earthly wealth and riches to dwell in poverty. *Jesus gave up his advantage to be served by all, that he might serve all by his death on the cross.*

Heavenly Father, continually remind us that your Son refrained from using his advantage as God incarnate to benefit himself and instead used it to benefit us. Amen.

FOR FURTHER REFLECTION, READ PHILIPPIANS 2:1–11.

The Perfect Neighbor

BUT HE, DESIRING TO JUSTIFY HIMSELF, SAID TO JESUS, "AND WHO IS MY NEIGHBOR?" JESUS REPLIED, "A MAN WAS GOING DOWN FROM JERUSALEM TO JERICHO, AND HE FELL AMONG ROBBERS, WHO STRIPPED HIM AND BEAT HIM AND DEPARTED, LEAVING HIM HALF DEAD."

Luke 10:29-30

Jesus delivered one of his most familiar parables in conversation with an expert in religious law. The lawyer, like we so often do, entered the conversation in an attempt to justify his works as worthy of eternal life. "I know the Law, and I love those worthy to be loved: my neighbors (i.e., the Jew who also knows the Law and keeps it as I do)." But Jesus pulls the rug out from under both him and us.

Jesus's closing words of the parable often throw us off. When Jesus says, *"You go, and do likewise,"* we assume him to be saying, "Go and be merciful, as the Law commands." It would seem that Jesus still asks the impossible since we cannot do so in any capacity near perfection. We know we can't earn salvation by works of the Law; so what is Jesus commanding? What is he telling us to go and do likewise?

Jesus asks us, not to be the Good Samaritan but the man as good as dead. He asks us to go and do *the* only thing we can: receive the work of the Good Samaritan, because in our sin, we're already dead. In the story of the Good Samaritan, we are the one stripped, beaten, and robbed. We are the one passed by the Law (the priest and Levite) on the other side of the road believed to be beyond saving. It is Christ who is the Good Samaritan.

In the glorious and great exchange of the gospel, Christ proved to be your neighbor and mine. Christ went and did like the Good Samaritan. Christ binds up our wounds through his on the cross. Christ anoints us with the oil of his Spirit; he purifies us with the wine of his blood shed for the forgiveness of our sins. Christ saddles us on the animal of his own righteous and life-giving works and brings us to safety. Christ pays our medical bills. And Christ promises to return for us.

> **Christ takes those who were beaten and left for dead by the Law (read us) and raises them to new life in him. He takes our guilt, our sin, and our shame on himself as he covers our naked, bloody souls in his righteousness, his perfection, and his eternal life. While the Law demands we be the neighbor, the gospel declares it is Christ who is our neighbor.**

Heavenly Father, thank you for binding our sin-caused wounds and for covering the cost of our healing and recovery with your body and blood. Amen.

FOR FURTHER REFLECTION, READ LUKE 10:25–37.

Scripture Speaks with an Accent

CHRIST REDEEMED US FROM THE CURSE OF THE LAW BY BECOMING A CURSE FOR US...SO THAT IN CHRIST JESUS THE BLESSING OF ABRAHAM MIGHT COME TO THE GENTILES, SO THAT WE MIGHT RECEIVE THE PROMISED SPIRIT THROUGH FAITH.

Galatians 3:13-14

When we claim that Christ is the high point of scripture, what does that mean? Paul gives the answer in Galatians 3:13-14. Did you miss it? Don't worry. Martin Luther, in his commentary on Galatians, points out what we fail to notice. "Paul does **not** say that Christ was made a curse for himself. The accent is on the two words '*for us*'" (emphasis added).

Implicit in the claim of Christ's centrality to scripture is that Christ is *for you*. Yes, you. He's not for some imaginary, perfect person. And he's not just for Abraham, Moses, David, Peter, or Paul. Christ is also *for you*.

But how do I know? Once again, Paul's letter to the Galatians delivers the answer: "Grace to you and peace from God our Father and the Lord Jesus Christ, who gave himself for our sins to deliver us from the present evil age according to the will of our God and Father" (1:3-4).

And once more, Luther draws attention to what Paul *doesn't* say. "He does not say, 'Who received our works,' but 'who gave.' Gave what? Not gold, or silver... but himself. What for? Not for a crown, or a kingdom, or our goodness, but *for our sins*" (emphasis added).[5]

We know Christ is for us because he gave himself. He took on the flesh and blood of a humanity who rejected him. He entered into time and space, into history, and gave himself to death on the cross for our sins. It was not for our best but for our worst. Christ gave himself, not merely for imaginary, "*little*" mistakes but for the mountainous, life-altering, relationship-ending sin ingrained in us. "Whatever sin I, you, all of us have committed or shall commit, they are Christ's sins as if he had committed them himself."[6]

Scripture speaks with an accent. It says Jesus became every sin we've ever committed. He bore the curse of all sin, of all people, of all time. "Christ also suffered once for sins, the righteous for the unrighteous, that he might bring us to God, being put to death in the flesh but made alive in the spirit" (1 Peter 3:18).

> **The accent scripture speaks with says, "Christ changes places with us. He gets our sins, we get his holiness."** [7]

Heavenly Father, we thank you for sending your Son to take on our sin and giving us his holiness. Amen.

FOR FURTHER REFLECTION, READ GALATIANS 3:1–18.

---

[5] RJ Grunewald, Galatains: Selections from Martin Luther's Commentary, 2015. 15.
[6] Grunewald, Galatains, 41.
[7] Grunewald, Galatains, 42.

Carried to the Table of the King

MEPHIBOSHETH!...DO NOT FEAR, FOR I WILL SHOW KINDNESS FOR THE SAKE OF YOUR FATHER JONATHAN, AND I WILL RESTORE TO YOU ALL THE LAND OF SAUL YOUR FATHER, AND YOU SHALL EAT AT MY TABLE ALWAYS.

2 Samuel 9:6-7

Mephibosheth was the victim of circumstance and timing. He was the grandson of Saul—the man who tried to kill David. When Saul and Jonathan died in battle against the Philistines, power shifted to David. Mephibosheth "was five years old when the news about Saul and Jonathan came ... and his nurse took him up and fled, and as she fled in her haste, he fell and became lame" (2 Samuel 4:4).

Mephibosheth didn't collude with Saul to end David's life. Yet, Mephibosheth carried the consequences of his grandfather's actions. What power Mephibosheth could have possessed, he lost while he was still a powerless child. His identity was a threat to his life. He couldn't outrun it or hide from it. Worse still, he was called to stand before his greatest enemy, King David—the one who held the power and control over his life.

Mephibosheth fell on his face before the king. He lay before his greatest enemy, lame from injuries of the past. He couldn't run or hide. He couldn't stand or fight. He could only fall before the king in fear.

Instead of destroying him, David restored him. He commanded Mephibosheth to eat at the table of the king who was once his enemy, like a member of the royal family. All this was not because he did anything to deserve it but because of who his father was.

> **We are Mephibosheth, made lame by the sin inherited by the fall of Adam and Eve. The Law calls us before the King of kings. We cannot run or hide. We cannot stand or fight. We know our guilt and failure. Yet to our amazement Jesus—the King of kings and Lord of hosts—says, "Do not be afraid" (Luke 5:10).**

In Christ, the new and better David, we are redeemed from our lame condition of sin. More than that, Jesus's life, death, and resurrection carry us to our place at God's table forever. We are not tolerated enemies for personal gain. We are more than friends. We eat at God's table as his children. We are brothers and sisters of Christ, family members and fellow heirs of the promised eternal life.

Heavenly Father, thank you for carrying us to your table to dine with you forever as your forgiven and redeemed children. Amen.

FOR FURTHER REFLECTION, READ 2 SAMUEL 9:1–11.

The Lord Who Remembers Not

"REMEMBER NOT THE SINS OF MY YOUTH OR
MY TRANSGRESSIONS; ACCORDING TO YOUR
STEADFAST LOVE REMEMBER ME, FOR THE SAKE
OF YOUR GOODNESS, O LORD!"

Psalm 25:7

Genesis 8:1 begins, "But God remembered Noah and all the beasts and all the livestock that were with him in the ark." Wait. Did God tell Noah to build an ark, send a flood to destroy the remaining living things on the earth, and then forget him? This is not the only time scripture speaks of God remembering. He also remembered Abraham, Rachel, Israel, Hannah, and so on. But why? Did he forget them at one time or another? Is that even possible? When scripture says "God remembered," what does that mean?

Chad Bird, on an episode of the podcast *40 Minutes in the Old Testament*, offers an answer: when scripture talks about God remembering something, it is not a mental exercise. For God to remember is for God to act. We remember birthdays, anniversaries, and other major life events with action, not just mere mental recall. Likewise, when scripture speaks of God remembering, it is for God to act toward the object of his remembrance.

Just as significant is the converse: if for God to remember is for him to act, then, for God to not remember is for him not to act. This plays out in the words of one of those crucified with Christ: "Jesus, remember me when you come into your kingdom" (Luke 23:42). He wasn't asking for Jesus to reminisce or reflect on his existence and the time they shared being crucified together. No, like David's prayer in Psalm 25:7, he asked Jesus not to act toward him according to his sin, but according to God's steadfast love and goodness on display right in front of him.

Christ's incarnation is God's ultimate act of remembering us according to his steadfast love. It is in Christ's coming that God's words through the prophet Jeremiah are fulfilled. "For I will forgive their iniquity, and I will remember their sin no more" (Jeremiah 31:34).

> **God remembered our sin, acting against it once and for all on Christ at his crucifixion. He forgave us and remembers our sin no more. By Christ's incarnation, his death, and his resurrection, he remembers us not according to our sins and transgressions but according to his goodness, acted out in Christ for us.**

Heavenly Father, remember not my sins and transgression; instead, remember me according to your steadfast love in Christ. Amen.

FOR FURTHER REFLECTION, READ LUKE 23:32–43.

THIRD WEEK *of* LENT

Anointed

MARY THEREFORE TOOK A POUND OF EXPENSIVE OINTMENT MADE FROM PURE NARD, AND ANOINTED THE FEET OF JESUS AND WIPED HIS FEET WITH HER HAIR. THE HOUSE WAS FILLED WITH THE FRAGRANCE OF THE PERFUME.

John 12:3

To a weary band of disciples, the home of Mary and Martha was an oasis on their yearly pilgrimage to the Holy City. The Passover was fast approaching, which meant Jesus, along with his disciples, were making their way to the City of Kings to commemorate Israel's deliverance. As Jesus reclined at the table enjoying the company of his friends, the room was unexpectedly filled with a rich fragrance.

With broken pieces of alabaster by Jesus's feet, all eyes turned to Mary as she knelt before her Lord. Jesus, the Son of God, was not anointed by a high government official, the high priest, or a religious figure. He was worshiped by a lowly, sinful woman wiping oil from his feet with her hair.

Mary poured out an offering of potent perfume and humility on the feet of Jesus. But it was not her costly gift to her Lord by which she found favor with God. Christ's costly gift of his very life and death in our place is the source of salvation, our favor with God. The feet that were drenched in fine oil would soon be drenched in his own blood. Jesus, to whom she had just poured out her wealth, would soon be poured out for her.

> **Every drop of our sin was poured out on Jesus as he was anointed with our transgressions. Our Lord willingly took the stench of our sin and death so we could enjoy the sweet balm of his righteousness and life.**

Our servant King trades places with us. It is Jesus who anoints us in our baptisms, not with fine oil but with simple water and the word. Jesus sanctifies us in the baptismal waters with his righteousness and crowns us with everlasting life.

Heavenly Father, your Son was poured out as an offering for our transgressions. Increase our faith and thanksgiving for what you have done for us so we may pour out our lives in loving service to our neighbor. Amen.

FOR FURTHER REFLECTION, READ PSALM 23.

Crowned

THEN PILATE TOOK JESUS AND FLOGGED HIM.
AND THE SOLDIERS TWISTED TOGETHER A
CROWN OF THORNS AND PUT IT ON HIS HEAD
AND ARRAYED HIM IN A PURPLE ROBE. THEY
CAME UP TO HIM, SAYING, "HAIL, KING OF THE
JEWS!" AND STRUCK HIM WITH THEIR HANDS.

John 19:1-3

On a Thursday night, a Roman courthouse beheld a coronation
of a king. Cloaked with a fine purple robe, he was adorned not
with an ornamental crown but with an array of thorns fashioned
by soldiers. He stood before a courtroom, mocked, abused, and
bleeding for the very ones he loved.

**Jesus was crowned not with gold or silver but with
the curse of the fall. On that Thursday night, Jesus
did not experience the adoration he justly deserved
but the punishment our sins warranted. In his
suffering and death for us, Jesus was crowned as
our King, and in so doing, he took up our sin, shame,
curse, and death for us. He bore the curse of sin in
our place.**

The wages of sin is death. We merited a crown of thorns and a payment of death, but in his grace and mercy, Jesus exchanges our crown of death for his crown of life. Jesus took upon himself our death so we may have life in him. Our King coronates us as heirs to his kingdom as he places upon our heads the watery word. He took the curse of our fall upon himself and gives us his blessing of life.

Heavenly Father, you have covered us with the royal robe of your righteousness and have made us heirs of eternal life. Give us faith to receive your gifts with joy. Amen.

> **FOR FURTHER REFLECTION, READ GENESIS 3:17–18.**

Life in the Blood

FOR THE LIFE OF THE FLESH IS IN THE BLOOD,
AND I HAVE GIVEN IT FOR YOU ON THE ALTAR
TO MAKE ATONEMENT FOR YOUR SOULS, FOR
IT IS THE BLOOD THAT MAKES ATONEMENT
BY THE LIFE.

Leviticus 17:11

Spend some time in the divine service of the Old Testament, especially in the book of Leviticus, and what you will find is a book dripping with blood. The heart of worship for the saints of the Old Testament is blood sacrifice.

Without a blood sacrifice, there can be no atonement for sins. Week after week, year after year, generation after generation, the blood of innocent animals was shed in the stead of sinners. The life of an animal was poured out for the transgressions of another. In the Lord's mercy, he gave his people these sacrifices whereby they would be cleansed from their iniquities and declared holy in his sight.

These sacrifices promised remission of sins on the account of the blood and life of another. Blood dripping from Jewish altars continually cried for Israel's forgiveness. Hymn writer Stephen Starke comments on this when he writes, "What these sacrifices promised from a God who sought to bless, Came at last a second Adam, priest and King of righteousness: Son of God, incarnate Savior, Son of Man, both Christ and Lord, who in naked shame would offer on the cross his blood outpoured."[8]

> From the wooden altar of the cross, the blood of Christ, our great High Priest, cries out for the remission of our sins. The blood of Jesus, our substitute, makes atonement for our sins through his perfect life and innocent death in our stead. Our great High Priest does not offer a blood sacrifice of a goat but he himself is our sacrifice. The Old Testament is centered around one thing—Jesus and him crucified for our forgiveness. He cleanses us from our iniquities with his own blood, once and for all.

Heavenly Father, you have made atonement for our sins on the altar of the cross. Preserve us in this gift so we may eternally live in you. Amen.

FOR FURTHER REFLECTION, READ MATTHEW 26:26–29.

---

[8] Starke, Stephen P. Lutheran Service Book. Pew Edition ed. Saint Louis, MO: Concordia Publishing House, 2006. 572

Our Scapegoat

AND AARON SHALL LAY BOTH HIS HANDS ON
THE HEAD OF THE LIVE GOAT, AND CONFESS
OVER IT ALL THE INIQUITIES OF THE PEOPLE
OF ISRAEL, AND ALL THEIR TRANSGRESSIONS,
ALL THEIR SINS. AND HE SHALL PUT THEM ON
THE HEAD OF THE GOAT AND SEND IT AWAY
INTO THE WILDERNESS BY THE HAND OF A MAN
WHO IS IN READINESS. THE GOAT SHALL BEAR
ALL THEIR INIQUITIES ON ITSELF TO A REMOTE
AREA, AND HE SHALL LET THE GOAT GO FREE
IN THE WILDERNESS.

Leviticus 16:21-22

The pinnacle of the church year for the Jewish people was
the Day of Atonement, a day centered around confession and
forgiveness. In the Old Testament blood sacrifices would be
made throughout the year to atone or pay for sin. However, this
day, the Day of Atonement, was different.

In addition to the blood sacrifice, a goat was chosen to bear the
sin of the people. Aaron, the high priest, laid his hands on the
goat, confessing the transgressions of the people. Weighed down

by their iniquities, the goat would then be led into the wilderness to die along with the sins of the people.

> **In Christ, our Day of Atonement has come once and for all. Isaac Watts beautifully portrays this in a hymn when he writes, "My faith would lay its hand on that dear head of Thine, While as a penitent I stand, And there confess my sin."[9] Jesus, our scapegoat, bears our sin and takes our confession, our guilt, our shame, and our transgressions upon himself to be led out into the wilderness of Calvary.**

We are free to confess because we no longer bear the punishment for our sins. Our sin, along with its punishment, was placed on Jesus. He took responsibility for the wrong we have done and the good we have left undone. Jesus has freed us from working for our salvation. Through the work of the Holy Spirit, we are given the gift of faith to believe the words of forgiveness and look to Christ, the one who takes away the sin of the world.

Heavenly Father, bring us to a daily repentance of our sin, and take away our guilt. Grant us peace through your words of forgiveness. Amen.

FOR FURTHER REFLECTION, READ HEBREWS 10:1–18.

---

[9] Watts, Isaac. Lutheran Service Book. Pew Edition ed. Saint Louis, MO: Concordia Publishing House, 2006. 431

Our Judgment

HE CALLS TO THE HEAVENS ABOVE AND TO
THE EARTH, THAT HE MAY JUDGE HIS PEOPLE:
"GATHER TO ME MY FAITHFUL ONES, WHO
MADE A COVENANT WITH ME BY SACRIFICE!"
THE HEAVENS DECLARE HIS RIGHTEOUSNESS,
FOR GOD HIMSELF IS JUDGE!

Psalm 50:4-6

Throughout the scriptures, the Lord gives us a glimpse into his glorious nature through the names he chooses for himself. Isaiah can't seem to find enough names to accurately describe the wonder of the Lord when he writes of our, "Wonderful Counselor, Mighty God, Everlasting Father, Prince of Peace" (Isaiah 9:6).

Names such as these fill us with comfort. They describe the work of the Lord—who he is and will always be for us. But what about the names the psalmists contribute to God? In Psalm 50, the poet names God as judge. How does that name comfort us?

Lent is all about the work of Jesus *for you*. Likewise, God's judgment is all about Jesus *for you*. Pastor Norman Nagel describes God's work as judge in this way: "God did the judgment on you when he did the judgment for your sins on Jesus. That death for your sin was given you."[10]

> **We have been judged as righteous because of Christ's life, death, and resurrection in our place.**

Through word and sacrament we are continually given the judgement of God, forgiven for the sake of Christ. He himself made a covenant with us. The gavel has fallen in our favor, and we are declared holy, beloved children of our heavenly Father. God himself is judge, and what a merciful judge he is!

Heavenly Father, in your beloved Son, you have judged us according to his righteousness and have judged him according to our sin. Comfort us with this promise as we ponder your love for us this Lent. Amen.

FOR FURTHER REFLECTION, READ PSALM 51.

---

[10] Nagel, Norman. Selected Sermons of Norman Nagel: From Valparaiso to St. Louis. Saint Louis, MO: Concordia Publishing House, 2004. 103

Our Gracious Gardener

I AM THE TRUE VINE, AND MY FATHER IS THE VINEDRESSER. EVERY BRANCH IN ME THAT DOES NOT BEAR FRUIT HE TAKES AWAY, AND EVERY BRANCH THAT DOES BEAR FRUIT HE PRUNES, THAT IT MAY BEAR MORE FRUIT. ...I AM THE VINE; YOU ARE THE BRANCHES. WHOEVER ABIDES IN ME AND I IN HIM, HE IT IS THAT BEARS MUCH FRUIT, FOR APART FROM ME YOU CAN DO NOTHING.

John 15:1–2, 5

Open the scriptures and you will find a theme running rampant. God seems always to be at work in gardens. They become classrooms in which God teaches and reveals himself to us. The Law and gospel are the tools in the hands of our gracious gardener that he uses to prune and nourish us. The scriptures are a nursery for our souls in which our heavenly Father tends to us.

In John 15, Jesus uses the illustration of a vine, branches, and gardener to teach us about our heavenly Father. It would be a beautiful parable if we could only erase one little detail. The first part makes us uncomfortable.

Cutting sounds painful, and more often than not, it is very painful. The daily cutting away and death of the Old Adam through the work of the Law is an agonizing process. Our sinful nature strains to create its own fruit. As sinners we do not want to freely take the life-giving nourishment of the vine. We want our own works, our own fruit, our own tree. "Mine" is the old Adam's favorite word. Our gracious gardener continually prunes us. He cuts away at the weeds of sin and unbelief to which we cling. Our heavenly Father daily cuts away at our old Adam.

> **On the tree of the cross, Christ takes our rotting fruit. Jesus takes our sin away from us and says, "Mine." Jesus is the branch that was cut off in our place so we might live. He takes what is ours so we may have what is his. Martin Luther writes, "For Christ is mine with his suffering, death, and life; the Holy Spirit, with his comfort; and the Father himself, with all his grace."[11] This is the comfort of the great exchange. Christ is mine, and I am his.**

Heavenly Father, you have grafted us into the true vine and nourish us with your life-giving word and sacrament. Cut away our sin and unbelief so we may be drawn to you alone for life and salvation. Amen.

FOR FURTHER REFLECTION, READ JOHN 15:1–17.

---

[11] Luther, Martin. Sermons on the Gospel of St. John Chapters 14-16. American Edition ed. Vol. 24. Luther's Works. Saint Louis, MO: Concordia Publishing House, 1961. 292

Named

FOR OUR SAKE HE MADE HIM TO BE SIN WHO KNEW NO SIN, SO THAT IN HIM WE MIGHT BECOME THE RIGHTEOUSNESS OF GOD.

2 Corinthians 5:21

A conscience haunted by sin is a conscience bound by fear. Fear, after all, is a natural product of sin. Martin Luther knew what it was to be haunted day and night. He was haunted by sin, death, and the power of the devil. The darkness knew his name. The slithering foe daily emerged from darkness, whispering his name, calling him by his sin.

The same darkness that haunted Luther haunts you and me. The serpent whispers our name. Our own sin is the fare that feeds the prowling lion that seeks to devour us. The devil knows our name and labels us by our sin. The devil breathes out death as he names us for what we are: sinners.

However, the final word does not belong to our sin or the haunting accusations of the serpent. The final word, unlike the voice of the serpent, does not whisper. It speaks in a loud voice. It is a voice that pierces through the darkness. This voice cries out in the midst of our darkness, "It is finished." This word broke into our darkness to take our sin, death, and fear, robbing the accuser of his power. The Lamb of God became our substitute. He became our sin. He became the one haunted by our sin.

> So, as Martin Luther writes, "When the devil throws our sins up to us and declares that we deserve death and hell, we ought to speak thus: 'I admit that I deserve death and hell. What of it?... For I know One who suffered and made satisfaction in my behalf. His name is Jesus Christ, the Son of God. Where he is, there I shall be also.'"[12] Our Lord does not name us according to our sin but names us according to what he has done for us. He calls us baptized, children of God, saints, his beloved.

Heavenly Father, you promised that you will never leave us or forsake us. Be with us as we meditate on the cross and marvel at your work for us. Amen.

FOR FURTHER REFLECTION, READ ISAIAH 53.

---

[12] Martin Luther, in Theodore G. Tappert, editor, *Luther: Letters of Spiritual Counsel* (Philadelphia, 1955), pages 86-87.

FOURTH WEEK *of* LENT

From Adored to Abhorred

AND AS MOSES LIFTED UP THE SERPENT IN THE WILDERNESS, SO MUST THE SON OF MAN BE LIFTED UP.

John 3:14

Israel's journey through the wilderness was characterized by distrust. Though the great I AM proved to be with them at every turn, when the going got tough, their faith got up and left. Though the Lord provided for their every need, they grumbled at every hardship they perceived.

As they followed God's command to travel the long way to avoid the land of Edom, the Israelites became impatient. They grumbled their stock line: "Why have you brought us up out of Egypt to die in the wilderness? For there is no food and no water, and we loathe this worthless food" (Numbers 21:5). The Lord sent poisonous serpents. As death visited the people through the fangs of the serpent, they realized their error. "We have sinned, for we have spoken against the LORD and against you. Pray to the LORD, that he take away the serpents from us" (Numbers 21:7).

Moses interceded. God instructed him to do something offensive and contrary to their religious sensibilities. "Make a fiery serpent and set it on a pole, and everyone who is bitten, when he sees it, shall live" (Numbers 21:8). Moses made and erected an image of the consequences for their sin, and all who looked at it lived.

> Jesus's words in John's gospel reveal the deeper meaning of this story in Israel's history. Jesus says he takes the place of the serpent and that he must necessarily do so. Paul, in his second letter to the Corinthians, puts this in familiar terms: "For our sake he made him to be sin who knew no sin, so that in him we might become the righteousness of God" (5:21).

Jesus became the embodiment of our sin and mistakes. He took in himself all our sin: our acts of injustice, our taking advantage of others for our gain, and our self-centered faithlessness. He, who was once adored by many, became an image abhorred by all. Yet, our salvation lies with him, the one who "redeemed us from the curse of the law by becoming a curse for us" (Galatians 3:13). It is there, as we behold the sight of our enfleshed sin, beaten, pierced, and crucified, that God calls us to look and live.

Heavenly Father, you sent your Son to become that which you most despise. Continually draw our eyes to Christ crucified for us, that we may live. Amen.

FOR FURTHER REFLECTION, READ JOHN 3:14–21.

The Ultimate Rejection

MY GOD, MY GOD, WHY HAVE YOU FORSAKEN ME? WHY ARE YOU SO FAR FROM SAVING ME, FROM THE WORDS OF MY GROANING?

Psalm 22:1

Few Psalms carry the gravitas of Psalm 22. Laden with Messianic themes, it bears a heavy load of cross-centered theology. We see this evidenced by Jesus as he quotes Psalm 22:1 from the cross. "And at the ninth hour Jesus cried with a loud voice, 'Eloi, Eloi, lema sabachthani?' which means, 'My God, my God, why have you forsaken me?'" (Mark 15:34).

> **We often feel the weight of these words in our own lives. In our pain and our loss, we cry out with the psalmist, "How long, O LORD? Will you forget me forever? How long will you hide your face from me?" (Psalm 13:1). "Lord, where is your steadfast love of old?" (Psalm 89:49). Our cries of suffering echo the words Jesus himself echoed. "My God, why have you forsaken me?"**

The trials and tribulations we experience in this broken world can cause us to feel abandoned by God. But Christ's incarnation demonstrates the opposite. God has neither left us, nor has he forsaken us. He has not excluded us. Though we deserved abandonment, it was Christ who took on our cosmic rejection. *Though we earned exclusion, it was Christ who was excluded for us.* In doing so, he provided us with the everlasting presence of God.

Heavenly Father, thank you for sending your dear Son to take on a forsakenness we could not handle so we can forever live in your presence. Amen.

FOR FURTHER REFLECTION, READ PSALM 22.

The New and Better Jonah

FOR JUST AS JONAH WAS THREE DAYS AND THREE NIGHTS IN THE BELLY OF THE GREAT FISH, SO WILL THE SON OF MAN BE THREE DAYS AND THREE NIGHTS IN THE HEART OF THE EARTH.

Matthew 12:40

Jonah was a racist. He hated the people of Nineveh, the capital city of Israel's nemesis, Assyria. God called Jonah to warn them of their impending destruction. He ran in the opposite direction—quite possibly out of fear, but certainly out of hatred. Yet, despite Jonah's character, Jesus attached himself to Jonah and his story—not to confer some high status upon Jonah but to perfect what Jonah did so poorly.

Jonah often enjoys a lofty status among the people found in the Old Testament. His book is short and narrative-based. It's easy to read and easy to teach to children. Many Christians equate his actions with childish antics. *"Silly Jonah! Don't you know you can't run from God?"* But Jonah's words in chapter 4 betray this sentiment: "O LORD, is not this what I said when I was yet in my country? That is why I made haste to flee to Tarshish; for I knew that you are a gracious God and merciful, slow to anger and abounding in steadfast love, and relenting from disaster" (v. 2). Jonah despised God showing mercy to those he hated.

But instead of distancing himself from Jonah, Jesus painted himself in Jonah's shadow. He too was a prophet sent by God with a message of warning to an enemy that hated him. Just as Jonah slept through a mighty storm, Jesus's friends caught him napping while they bucketed water out of their storm-tossed ship. And just like Jonah was buried in the belly of the fish for three days, so too was Jesus buried for three days in the heart of the earth. Though Jesus connected himself to Jonah in his actions, he did so as Jonah's opposite. Jesus did not run away. He came to lay down his life for those who hated him. He did so, not out of reluctance and hatred but willingly and out of love. *Jesus did not despise God for showing us mercy but came as the instrument of that mercy.*

> **Jesus, the Son of God, supersedes Jonah as the new and better prophet sent to his enemies. He came not just as the messenger of God's unrelenting mercy but as the message itself.**

Heavenly Father, you mercy knows no bounds. Continue to keep us in your relentless mercy and grace shown in Christ. Amen.

FOR FURTHER REFLECTION, READ MATTHEW 12:38–42.

The Extraordinary for the Ordinary

BUT GOD CHOSE WHAT IS FOOLISH IN THE WORLD TO SHAME THE WISE; GOD CHOSE WHAT IS WEAK IN THE WORLD TO SHAME THE STRONG; GOD CHOSE WHAT IS LOW AND DESPISED IN THE WORLD, EVEN THINGS THAT ARE NOT, TO BRING TO NOTHING THINGS THAT ARE.

1 Corinthians 1:27–28

Leading up to Jesus's birth, God used ordinary (and downright sinful) people and events to accomplish his greatest purpose. Four out of the five women mentioned in Jesus's genealogy in Matthew had sordid histories. Yet they are part of Jesus's family line. Jesus attached himself to these people and shared flesh, blood, and genes with them.

Tamar, seeking revenge, dressed as a prostitute and tricked her father-in-law, Judah, into sleeping with her. She conceived and had twins (Genesis 38). God used the oldest of these two socially illegitimate children, Perez, to carry on the blessing and promise given to Abraham (Genesis 12:1–2).

Rahab, a prostitute of Jericho, hid the spies Joshua sent from the men of Jericho. As a result, she and all in her house were saved from the destruction of the city. More than that, God included her in Jesus's family line. Rahab would marry Salmon (the great-great-great-grandson of Perez) and give birth to Boaz (Matthew 1:3).

Boaz married Ruth, a foreign, gentile widow, redeeming her and her mother-in-law out of destitution. Boaz and Ruth fathered Obed, who fathered Jesse, who fathered David. David, the shepherd boy turned king (Matthew 1:5-6a), fathered Solomon by Bathsheba, the wife of Uriah (Matthew 1:6b). David had Uriah killed to cover up his affair with Bathsheba after she became pregnant.

Eventually, God came to an unmarried virgin in a backwater town in middle of nowhere Galilee. He chose her to be the mother of his only begotten Son, who would be the crucified Savior of the world (Luke 1:26-38; 2:1-21).
God exchanged the extraordinary in the world to work through the ordinary. He united himself to the regular flesh and blood of humanity. Jesus died the painful, ordinary death of an insurrectionist. Jesus was defeated and killed by ordinary humans. Yet, *Jesus's seemingly ordinary death absolved the world of its sins and brought forgiveness to all—to us.*

Heavenly Father, you continually exchange the extraordinary to use the ordinary to show us your power. Thank you for coming to us in the ordinary flesh and blood of humanity so we can know you. Amen.

FOR FURTHER REFLECTION, READ 1 CORINTHIANS 1:26-31.

A Fiery Exchange

I BAPTIZE YOU WITH WATER, BUT HE WHO IS
MIGHTIER THAN I IS COMING ... HE WILL BAPTIZE
YOU WITH THE HOLY SPIRIT AND WITH FIRE.

Luke 3:16

In Luke 3:16, John the Baptizer speaks some unsettling words about Jesus. Baptized with fire? That doesn't sound good. But as with all things regarding Christ, it's wonderfully more than it appears to be.

> **The baptism we receive, Christ first took upon himself. At his baptism, the Holy Spirit descended upon him. Jesus took humanity's place as he began his journey to a second baptism (Luke 12:50). It was a baptism of blood and of judgment as he hung in our place. He endured a baptism of fire as he incurred the full wrath of God in our stead.**

Like the fourth man with Shadrach, Meshach, and Abednego, Christ willingly entered the fiery furnace of God's judgment with us and for us. He didn't join to watch us burn, bound by our sin. Instead, he sends us out unbound, unburned, and free from sin's stench while he stayed behind.

On the cross he took our old, sinful Adam into the flames of God's judgment. In return he gave us his resurrected and recreated Adam. He took our bindings and our punishment and gave us his clothing of righteousness and his freedom from sin. In our baptism, Christ takes our reeking, foul, and petulant sin-scented odor before God, washing it away. In exchange he gives us his sweet, soft, pleasing aroma. Christ's blood extinguishes the flames the old Adam earned. Our sinful stench goes up in smoke, blown away by the breath, the Spirit of God.

Heavenly Father, we thank you for sending your Son to extinguish the flames of your judgment against our sin by his blood. Amen.

FOR FURTHER REFLECTION, READ LUKE 12:49–53.

Our Great Worship Leader

FOR HE WHO SANCTIFIES AND THOSE WHO ARE SANCTIFIED ALL HAVE ONE SOURCE. THAT IS WHY HE IS NOT ASHAMED TO CALL THEM BROTHERS, SAYING, "I WILL TELL OF YOUR NAME TO MY BROTHERS; IN THE MIDST OF THE CONGREGATION I WILL SING YOUR PRAISE."

Hebrews 2:11-12

Jesus quotes the heavy words of Psalm 22:1 from the cross. "My God, my God, why have you forsaken me?" The rest of the Psalm slogs forward with graphic imagery of the suffering that Jesus would and did experience on the cross. But halfway through, the tone and imagery shift.

The writer of Hebrews puts the words of Psalm 22:22 in Jesus's mouth. Here, Jesus calls them (meaning us) his siblings, and he says he will lead us in praise. Jesus calls himself our worship leader.

Worship plays a personal part in our lives. In worship we meet with the divine creator of all things on a personal level.

In worship, we commune with fellow members of the body of Christ. In worship, we experience a foretaste of the promised eternal paradise, as we receive assurance of the forgiveness and salvation Jesus earned for us.

First and foremost, God serves us in worship. He comes to us in his word spoken and sung. He comes to us in water and word when a baptism takes place. He comes to us in a tangible way when we receive Jesus's body and blood in, with, and under the bread and wine of communion. In all of it, God works for us. He calls us together by his word. He gathers us together around his sacraments. He enlightens us with his gifts of faith, forgiveness, and salvation. He sanctifies and keeps us in that faith by the power of his Spirit.

> **Worship not only starts with God; it also returns to him through the filter of the cross. Jesus did not enter a cosmic retirement after his ascension. By his life, death, and resurrection, Jesus became our mediator (1 Timothy 2:5). The words we sing, say, and hear proclaim to us that Christ lived for us; that he died for us; and that he rose for us.**

The crucified and risen Christ acts as our rightful and best worship leader. He stands between us and God, exchanging the worship we so poorly perform for the worship he so perfectly lived.

Heavenly Father, we thank you that your Son perfects our imperfect worship. Amen.

FOR FURTHER REFLECTION, READ PSALM 22:22–31.

Our Silent Defense and Bloody Apology

"HAVE YOU NO ANSWER TO MAKE? SEE HOW MANY CHARGES THEY BRING AGAINST YOU." BUT JESUS MADE NO FURTHER ANSWER, SO THAT PILATE WAS AMAZED.

Mark 15:4-5

Jesus punctuated his ministry with words and teachings. However, Jesus remained uncharacteristically silent during his trials. The Son of Man, who seemed to have an answer for every question, spoke very little at a time when his words seemed most needed.

The words Jesus did speak offered no defense against the false witnesses, collusion, and conspiracy he faced before the religious leaders. He made no attempt to answer false accusations. Despite the lack of credible evidence, Jesus kept quiet. The high priest stood up. "Have you no answer to make? What is it that these men testify against you?" Still, his silence remained (Matthew 26:62-63). Jesus's silence persisted before the Roman governor, Pilate, as he echoed the high priest's questions.

Jesus's silent "defense" was not for his sake but for ours. *In not defending himself, Christ defended us*. The very words he spoke at his trial assured his death.

> *The high priest asked him, "Are you the Christ, the Son of the Blessed?" And Jesus said, "I am, and you will see the Son of Man seated at the right hand of Power, and coming with the clouds of heaven." And the high priest tore his garments and said, "What further witnesses do we need? You have heard his blasphemy. What is your decision?" And they all condemned him as deserving death. (Mark 14:61-64)*

On the cross, Jesus remained our defense. He bore the full wrath of God for the sin of every person—past, present, and future. That was why he came. Jesus never assumed his innocence, because on the cross he assumed our guilt. "He was oppressed, and he was afflicted, yet he opened not his mouth; like a lamb that is led to the slaughter, and like a sheep that before its shearers is silent, so he opened not his mouth" (Isaiah 53:7).

Furthermore, in assuming our guilt by not offering a reasoned defense, or apology (from the Greek apologia), of his innocence, Jesus offered up another kind of apology. This time, it was a bloody acknowledgment of our offenses and failures. "Father, forgive them" (Luke 23:34).

The incarnation of the Son of God was an apology tour. Except he didn't apologize for himself. He apologized for us. Instead of defending himself, Christ laid down his life in defense of ours as a double apology, both an admission of guilt and a defense against the wrath of God.

Heavenly Father, we thank you that in Christ's assumption of our guilt, we are declared innocent by his blood. Amen.

FOR FURTHER REFLECTION, READ MARK 14:53-65; 15:1-5.

FIFTH WEEK *of* LENT

Prove It

UNLESS I SEE IN HIS HANDS THE MARK OF THE NAILS, AND PLACE MY FINGER INTO THE MARK OF THE NAILS, AND PLACE MY HAND INTO HIS SIDE, I WILL NEVER BELIEVE.

John 20:25

Show me. If I'm going to believe, I need to be convinced—on my terms. After all, you know the saying: *fool me once, shame on you; fool me twice, shame on me.* So, provide the evidence.

Thomas was stubbornly determined. He believed Jesus was the Messiah and did not shy away from bold statements to support his conviction. Peter wasn't the only disciple who had tenacious confidence in Jesus. After all, it was Thomas, not Peter, who instructed his fellow disciples, "let us also go, that we may die with him" (John 11:16).

Thomas had seen all the miracles and wonders. His ears heard the voice of God. He had a front-row seat as Lazarus rose from the dead by only a few words from his teacher. But there was also something else he had seen. He had seen his teacher and friend taken away. He had seen Jesus murdered, dead, and buried.

The darkness of unbelief and doubt swirled around in Thomas's head like a storm. He locked himself away from the world with the other disciples. His faith certainly had wilted and shriveled up.

Like a broken record, the words of the religious leaders replayed in his head. "If you are the Son of God, come down from the cross." *Why didn't Jesus save himself? Why didn't Jesus fight for himself?* Maybe Jesus wasn't the Messiah they had thought he was.

The words, *"We have seen the Lord"* were not comforting to Thomas. They were salt in a fresh, deep wound. If Thomas was to ever believe again, there would need to be concrete proof.

> **Jesus did prove that he was the Son of God, though not according to the indignant stipulation of the religious leaders. He proved he was the Son of God, not by leaving the cross but by dying on it.**

Peace be with you ceaselessly flowed from the Savior's lips to doubting Thomas. Just as Jesus reached out to grab Peter as he sank beneath the stormy seas, the risen Jesus reached out his nail-pierced hand to comfort Thomas, sinking in the waves of unbelief.

Heavenly Father, we believe. Help our unbelief, and comfort our troubled consciences with the peace of your gospel. Amen.

FOR FURTHER REFLECTION, READ JOHN 20:24–29.

The Greater David

THEN DAVID SAID TO THE PHILISTINE, "YOU COME TO ME WITH A SWORD AND WITH A SPEAR AND WITH A JAVELIN, BUT I COME TO YOU IN THE NAME OF THE LORD OF HOSTS, THE GOD OF THE ARMIES OF ISRAEL, WHOM YOU HAVE DEFIED. THIS DAY THE LORD WILL DELIVER YOU INTO MY HAND, AND I WILL STRIKE YOU DOWN AND CUT OFF YOUR HEAD."

1 Samuel 17:45-46

From the rising of the sun until dusk, Israel was subjected to the taunts, jeers, and threats of their adversary. The words of the Philistines were hurled like rocks into the camp of the armies of Saul. As Israel shook in fear, enslaved to the ridicule of their opponent, a lowly shepherd boy stood in their midst. He was undeterred by the harassment of the Philistines. David stood confident, not in the strength of the army but in the efficacy of the word.

We, like the Israelite army, shake in fear as the devil taunts and threatens us. We cannot defend ourselves against our foe. We are captive to the powers of sin, death, and the devil. However, just as the shepherd boy, David, steps forth and speaks in the midst of terror-stricken armies, so our Good Shepherd, Christ, comes to us and speaks peace to terror-stricken consciences.

> **The hymn beautifully affirms our confidence, "As true as God's own word is true, not earth nor hell's satanic crew against us shall prevail. Their might? A joke, a mere facade! God is with us and we with God—Our vict'ry cannot fail."[13]**

Our David comes not to slay our enemies with a sling and some stones. Our David slays our enemy with his own death. He crushes the head of the serpent as he dies in our place on the cross. Our victory cannot fail. It is finished in Christ. It was won on the cross and given to us in word and sacrament.

Heavenly Father, when the threats of our enemies taunt us, speak to us through your word and remind us of the victory you have won for us. Strengthen us with your word and sacrament so we may remain steadfast in you. Amen.

FOR FURTHER REFLECTION, READ 1 JOHN 5:1–12.

---

[13] Fabricius, Jacob, and Catherine Winkworth. Lutheran Service Book. Pew Edition ed. Saint Louis, MO: Concordia Publishing House, 2006.666

Remembering to Forget

BEHOLD, I HAVE ENGRAVED YOU ON
THE PALMS OF MY HANDS.

Isaiah 49:16

The marks on our skin tell stories. Scars are visible reminders of our past—they are a part of life. While some scars are visible, others are not. Guilt and shame often dig into our hearts and leave their mark. The painful aftermath of our transgressions leaves us broken. Our souls become scarred and torn by sin. The wounds sin leaves in our lives are a reminder that we are sinners. The psalmist, David, knew his sin all too well. He could not forget his transgressions. Sin stood before him, testifying as a witness to his evil heart.

We can kneel in confession with David as he prays in the psalm, "For I know my transgressions and my sin is ever before me. Against you, you only, have I sinned and done what is evil in your sight" (Psalm 51:3-4). Our transgressions do more than just leave a little mark in remembrance of failure. They condemn us.

Yet, there is another one, a greater one, who bears scars left by sin. Jesus chose to bear scars. They are not accidental. He willingly took on our sin and with it, our death. God ascribed our iniquities to Christ. He felt the full sting and pain of our transgressions. He suffered the punishment and death that our sins held against us. The hands of God were inscribed with our sin. *We know our God by the wounds he sustained for us.*

Scars tell stories, and the scars of Christ are no different. His scars tell of a God of mercy, a God who would rather die in our place than condemn us. Our God remembers not our transgressions but his promised mercy. The scars of Christ tell of a God who walks with us, who suffers, bleeds, and dies for us. His scars do more than just tell a story; they plead for our forgiveness.

> **We, therefore, can confess: for I know my transgressions, but Christ is always before me.**

Heavenly Father, in the death of your beloved Son, you remember our sins no more. Grant us grace to forgive in the same way that you forgive. Let us die to our sinful nature and rise in your forgiveness and grace. Amen.

FOR FURTHER REFLECTION, READ PSALM 25.

Behold the Light of the World

AFTER THESE THINGS THE WORD OF
THE LORD CAME TO ABRAM IN A VISION:
"FEAR NOT, ABRAM, I AM YOUR SHIELD; YOUR
REWARD SHALL BE VERY GREAT." ...AND HE
BROUGHT HIM OUTSIDE AND SAID, "LOOK
TOWARD HEAVEN, AND NUMBER THE STARS,
IF YOU ARE ABLE TO NUMBER THEM." THEN
HE SAID TO HIM, "SO SHALL YOUR OFFSPRING
BE." AND HE BELIEVED THE LORD, AND HE
COUNTED IT TO HIM AS RIGHTEOUSNESS.

Genesis 15:1, 5-6

Uncertainty encircled Abraham. His circumstances indicated that his prayers had been either inaudible or forgotten. Abraham stepped out to see a sky glistening with stars. As God created light of out darkness, he spoke of a promised light into Abraham's darkness.

When fear and doubt threatened to overtake Abraham, the Lord drew near and comforted him. "Do not be afraid, Abram. I am your shield, your very great reward."

This sweet declaration Abraham received soothes ears scarred by sin and shame. We, like Abraham, are sinners. When we contemplate our own lives, we may wonder with Abraham if God is listening. When circumstances bring hopelessness, and when the accusations of the Law come, God's word comforts us with Jesus. "Fear not, for behold, I bring you good news of great joy" (Luke 2:10).

> **The Lord is merciful to Abraham. In promising him innumerable offspring, he uses the celestial lights of the night sky to illustrate the magnitude of the promise. The sky Abraham saw night after night became a canvas filled with shimmering promises.**

The heavens proclaimed the good news as they shepherded the Magi to Christ, the Light of the World. The star prophesied, "Behold the Light of the World who has come to take away the darkness of the world."

The bright Morning Star, the Prince of Peace, speaks gently to us and says, "Do not be afraid." Abraham looked up at a dark sky glittering with hope. We see the promised Light nailed to a cross, taking our darkness and giving us his light. Do not be afraid. The Light of the world reaches out with his nail-scarred hands and says, "Do not be afraid. I am your shield from danger and your righteousness. I am your very great reward."

Heavenly Father, you have sent your Son to take away our sin. Shine through our darkness with the light of Your gospel so we may trust in your sure promise.
Amen.

FOR FURTHER REFLECTION, READ MARK 15:33–39.

Climbing Trees with Jesus

AND WHEN JESUS CAME TO THE PLACE, HE
LOOKED UP AND SAID TO HIM, "ZACCHAEUS,
HURRY AND COME DOWN, FOR I MUST STAY
AT YOUR HOUSE TODAY."

Luke 19:5

An outcast already, by virtue of his job as chief tax collector of Jericho (read also, chief sinner), Zacchaeus lived in a perpetual state of humiliation. Yet, he willingly humiliated himself further by running ahead of the crowd. He heaped on more humiliation by climbing a tree. Picture it: a man, whose arms and legs aren't quite long enough, climbing a tree in a robe and sandals. It could not have been smooth or graceful. People noticed. As Jesus came to the tree, he didn't pass by. Instead, he called up. "Zacchaeus, hurry and come down, for I must stay at your house today" (Luke 19:5).

Jesus didn't call Zacchaeus down just to eat and stay with him. Jesus called Zacchaeus down because Zacchaeus couldn't stay up there. Salvation could not come to Zacchaeus if he stayed clinging to the branches of that sycamore tree.

As people like Zacchaeus, we live in a constant state of humiliation in our old Adams and old Eves. Our sinful natures get the better of us. We don't even understand our own actions. We don't do the good we want, and the evil we do not want, we keep on doing (Romans 7). We desperately cling to the branches of our own works and cover ourselves in leaves to hide our shame.

But also like Zacchaeus, Jesus doesn't leave us hanging. Instead, he reverses our humiliation. He calls us down. He tells us he must stay with us. In the ultimate act of humiliation, Jesus trades places with us. *Jesus calls us down and willingly climbs up the tree to hang in our place.* "For the Son of Man came to seek and to save the lost" (Luke 19:10).

> **On the cross, Jesus redeemed us by becoming the curse for sin (Galatians 3:13). He was beaten and bloodied, bearing the sins of humanity and the punishment we deserved. The cross of Christ, the tree on which he saved humanity, proclaims, "Truly, I say to you, today you will be with me in paradise" (Luke 23:43). "Today salvation has come to this house" (Luke 19:9).**

Heavenly Father, thank you for sending you Son to call us down from the trees of our works and to climb up in our place. Amen.

FOR FURTHER REFLECTION, READ LUKE 19:1-10.

A Defeated God

THEN HE SAID, "YOUR NAME SHALL NO LONGER BE CALLED JACOB, BUT ISRAEL, FOR YOU HAVE STRIVEN WITH GOD AND WITH MEN, AND HAVE PREVAILED."

Genesis 32:28

In the midst of Jacob's return home after twenty years of exile, a seemingly "ungodly" story appears in which Jacob wrestles with a man who later turns out to be God himself. As the sun rises, the man tries to depart. Jacob, realizing it is God, demands a blessing before he will let him go. The man consents, asking for Jacob's name. "Your name shall no longer be called Jacob, but Israel, for you have striven with God and with men, and have prevailed."

Did God just admit defeat? Did Jacob beat God? How does a mortal man with a dislocated hip (Genesis 32:25) prevail over the all-powerful Creator of the universe who spoke all life into existence? The simple answer: *God let him*.

That night, God condescended to be "equal" with humanity and let Jacob prevail over him. He rolled around in the sweat, grime, and dirt with the "dust of the earth" and allowed himself to be defeated.

It wouldn't be the last time he'd allow himself to be defeated. *God, through Christ, willingly let sinful humanity beat him, crucify him, and defeat him.* "I lay down my life that I may take it up again. No one takes it from me, but I lay it down of my own accord" (John 10:17b-18a).

> **After allowing Jacob to prevail over him, God blessed his victorious opponent. In the same way, we are the ones who receive the blessing in "defeating" God by Christ's death on the cross. God changes our names.**

Like Jacob to Israel, from "one who cheats" to "one who strives with God and prevails," our names are changed from *sinner to saint*, from *enemy* of God to *son* or *daughter* of God; and as a son or daughter, inheritors of eternal life.

Heavenly Father, we praise you that in your willingness to be defeated, you give us the ultimate blessing of being your children and heirs of eternal life. Amen.

FOR FURTHER REFLECTION, READ GENESIS 32:22-32.

Wearing Jesus's Wounds

THEN ISAAC SAID TO JACOB, "PLEASE COME NEAR, THAT I MAY FEEL YOU, MY SON, TO KNOW WHETHER YOU ARE REALLY MY SON ESAU OR NOT." SO JACOB WENT NEAR TO ISAAC HIS FATHER, WHO FELT HIM AND SAID, "THE VOICE IS JACOB'S VOICE, BUT THE HANDS ARE THE HANDS OF ESAU." AND HE DID NOT RECOGNIZE HIM, BECAUSE HIS HANDS WERE HAIRY LIKE HIS BROTHER ESAU'S HANDS. SO HE BLESSED HIM. HE SAID, "ARE YOU REALLY MY SON ESAU?" HE ANSWERED, "I AM."

Genesis 27:21-24

Prompted by his mother, Rebekah, Jacob dressed in his brother Esau's best garments. He covered his smooth arms and neck with the skin of a young goat to mimic Esau's hairy exterior. He took a meal prepared just the way his father liked it and played the part of his older brother. "I am Esau your firstborn" (Genesis 27:19).

Blind Isaac bid Jacob near. He felt the goat hair on Jacob's neck and arms. "The voice is Jacob's voice, but the hands are the hands of Esau" (Genesis 27:22). Isaac smelled the smell of Esau, but after the meal, he blessed Jacob.

Like Jacob before Isaac, you and I appear before God in the clothes of another. Jesus earned these garments by dwelling in our flesh on earth. He lived the perfect life, doing everything the Father commanded him. He died the death we should have died and rose again to new life. Christ washes our garments white with his blood, the blood of the Lamb (Revelation 7:14). We put on these garments, these robes of righteousness, in baptism. "For as many of you as were baptized into Christ have put on Christ" (Galatians 3:27).

Though our voices sound like ours, we smell of Christ's death and resurrection. Though our skin is smooth, Christ's wounds are felt on our hands and on our side. In baptism, God no longer compares our works to the works the Law demands. Instead, he sees Christ's perfect works as ours. *The Father sees us as he sees his firstborn and gives us the blessings he earned: forgiveness, righteousness, salvation, and eternal life.*

Heavenly Father, thank you for seeing us not in our ragged clothes of sinfulness, but in Christ's righteous robes that he earned for us by his life, death, and resurrection. Amen.

FOR FURTHER REFLECTION, READ GENESIS 27:1–24.

HOLY WEEK

CHRIST CRUCIFIED, DIED, BURIED, AND RAISED

for you

A Foal for a Steed

SAY TO THE DAUGHTER OF ZION, "BEHOLD, YOUR KING IS COMING TO YOU, HUMBLE, AND MOUNTED ON A DONKEY, ON A COLT, THE FOAL OF A BEAST OF BURDEN."

Matthew 21:5

Jesus's ride into Jerusalem showed he was not the Messiah many people expected. The title "Messiah" or "Christ" played a complicated role in first-century Israel. Expectations were high and as varied as their people were. "Is this him? Where's he from? Is now the time when the kingdom of Israel will be restored?"

Many expected that the Messiah would come to restore Israel by and to earthly power. He would lead the revolt and defeat the Roman occupiers of their holy land. He would bring back a time of independence and prosperity not seen since King David. As a victorious warrior and God-ordained king, he would usher in God's earthly reign with his ascent to the throne.

Great warriors rode horses. As the fastest means of transportation in those days, they served as symbols of power and might. They could move with great speed and strength. No earthly king in his right mind ever commanded, "Saddle up my war donkey!" But Jesus chose to ride in on a less than fully grown donkey—not as a symbol of war and might, but as a symbol of peace and humility.

> **In riding into Jerusalem on the foal of donkey, Jesus signaled something different. He would not bring peace by acts worthy of earthly glory. He would not obtain concord by chasing out foreign forces and assuming an earthly throne. He would achieve peace another way.**

Jesus's humble ride into the capital city of Israel showed he would achieve a peace that no earthly ruler could in the way that only God himself could. On Sunday, they praised him. By Friday, they called for his crucifixion. Though he was innocent, they found him guilty. *But by his death, Jesus brought us lasting peace—not as the world gives, but as only God could give, in the forgiveness of sin.*

Heavenly Father, keep us in the lasting peace you brought between us by your Son's death. Amen.

FOR FURTHER REFLECTION, READ MATTHEW 21:1–5.

The Holy Coal

"BEHOLD, THIS HAS TOUCHED YOUR LIPS;
YOUR GUILT IS TAKEN AWAY, AND YOUR
SIN ATONED FOR."

Isaiah 6:7

As *the* unique and powerful source of life, God stands above all else in his holiness. This spells danger for anyone or anything less than holy, including you and me. Our unholiness excludes us from God's presence. But Jesus changed that. "An unclean person was to keep away from God, but God in Christ sought out such a person."[14]

When God gave instructions for the tabernacle, he established a place where his holiness could reside called the Most Holy Place. Separated by a veil from the Holy Place, the ark of the covenant, God's mercy seat, rested there. God's holiness would kill any who entered—not because his holiness is bad but because it's so good. God permitted the high priest to enter his holy presence once a year and only after he became ritually purified.

Isaiah found himself standing terrified in God's presence (Isaiah 6). He knew his sinful nature was not compatible with God's holiness. But God did something remarkable. He sent a creature, called a seraphim, carrying a burning coal. The creature touched Isaiah's lips with the coal and declared him clean. God's holiness transformed Isaiah instead of destroying him. Normally, something clean became dirty when it touched something unclean. But the holy coal didn't become profane. Instead it made Isaiah clean and holy.

> **Jesus is the ultimate embodiment of Isaiah's holy coal. He touched a leper, and instead of becoming dirty himself, the leper became clean. He touched the dead body of a widow's son. Instead of becoming dead to God, he made the widow's son alive. Jesus does the same for us.**

Jesus touched humanity by becoming human. *By setting the holy coal of his crucified and risen body to the lips of sinful humanity*, Jesus took away our guilt. He forgave our sin and transformed us. Once we were dead. Now we're alive.

Heavenly Father, we thank you for sending us the holy coal of Christ to cleanse us from our unholiness and to bring us into your presence. Amen.

FOR FURTHER REFLECTION, READ ISAIAH 6:1–7.

---

[14] Arthur A. Luke 1:1-9:50. St. Louis: Concordia Pub. House, 1996. 312

A King for a Criminal

BUT THE CHIEF PRIESTS STIRRED UP
THE CROWD TO HAVE HIM RELEASE FOR
THEM BARABBAS INSTEAD.

Mark 15:11

No greater injustice exists than to declare the innocent guilty and the guilty innocent. For the one guilty of irreparable harm to walk off scot-free offends our conscience. But for the innocent one to pay for the crimes of the guilty assaults the very notions of truth, morality, and justice we hold dear. Still, all four gospel writers record for us this gravest of injustices.

Barabbas appeared as part of Pilate's last-ditch effort to save Jesus from the envy of the religious leaders. They had colluded and conspired to bring false testimony against Jesus. The evidence presented failed to prove Jesus's guilt. Pilate repeated that he couldn't find anything Jesus did worthy of death. Pilate's wife sent a message calling Jesus a righteous man. Even Herod Antipas found nothing wrong with Jesus.

So Pilate stood him next to Barabbas. He assumed, that in the shadow of the notorious and guilty Barabbas, Jesus's innocence would shine brighter. Barabbas was guilty of capital offenses. Not only was he guilty of murder, but he was also guilty of insurrection, a crime of the highest order in Rome. The punishment? Crucifixion.

But Pilate's plan failed. The voices of the religious leaders succeeded in subverting justice. "So Pilate decided that their demand should be granted. He released the man who had been thrown into prison for insurrection and murder, for whom they asked, but he delivered Jesus over to their will" (Luke 23:24-25).

Jesus suffered the gravest injustice at the hands of the peccant. Though innocent, he was traded for one guilty of the highest crimes. A king was exchanged for a criminal. But this exchange was not for murderous, rebellious Barabbas alone. *Jesus was traded for those who polluted justice; for those who sought to crucify an innocent man; for the ones who stood by in complicity. Jesus was traded for us.*

> **We are Barabbas. As insurrectionists, we rebelled against God's will. We tried to set up our own rule in God's place. We are guilty of murder. Our sin killed Jesus. But he willingly allowed himself to be traded, the innocent for the guilty, so we, like Barabbas, might be set free.**

Heavenly Father, we are the guilty ones. But despite our guilt, you sent your Son to trade places with us so we would be declared innocent as you are. Amen.

FOR FURTHER REFLECTION, READ MARK 15:6-15.

Pilate's Baptism

SO WHEN PILATE SAW THAT HE WAS GAINING NOTHING, BUT RATHER THAT A RIOT WAS BEGINNING, HE TOOK WATER AND WASHED HIS HANDS BEFORE THE CROWD, SAYING, "I AM INNOCENT OF THIS MAN'S BLOOD; SEE TO IT YOURSELVES."

Matthew 27:24

Pilate tried to get Jesus off the hook. He used everything in his power to show the chief priests and the crowd Jesus's innocence. He failed. But he saw relief—for himself anyway. Washing his hands, he declared himself innocent of Jesus's blood. Pilate absolved himself of Jesus's forthcoming death using a little water and some words. Pilate baptized himself.

With troubled consciences, we act like Pilate. We seek refuge and relief in our words and actions. We try harder to right everything we've done wrong. And when we fail, we try to stand at the font, sprinkle water on our heads, and hope to declare ourselves forgiven by our mediocre efforts. We try to baptize ourselves.

Washing in Pilate's baptism fails to cleanse any unrighteousness. It only whitewashes our exterior, and temporarily at best. Guilt remains in spite of self-justifying pronouncements. Garments stay stained despite self-righteous deeds (Isaiah 64:6). *We can't see to it ourselves.*

Like Pilate, we stand wearing blinders, looking down at our dirty hands. We fail to see Jesus standing next to us. We fail to hear his words. We miss Christ condemned, mocked, and beaten for us, who took our alms of greed and wickedness (Mark 7:1-23) to the cross in exchange for *his* righteousness.

Jesus says, "Give me your sins, and behold, everything is clean for you" (Luke 11:39-41). Be cleaned by the waters attached to my works ...

> *having been buried with [me] in baptism, in which you were also raised with [me] through the powerful working of God, who raised [me] from the dead. And you, who were dead in your trespasses... God made alive together with [me], having forgiven all [your] trespasses, by canceling the record of debt that stood against [you] with its legal demands. This [I] set aside, nailing it to the cross. (Colossians 2:12-14)*

He says, "Be washed in the waters attached to my name." "For these words, *'In the name of the Father and of the Son and of the Holy Spirit,' mean the Father, the Son, and the Holy Spirit are baptizing you*"[15]

Heavenly Father, thank you for sending your Son to take on that which we cannot see to ourselves: our unrighteousness, and giving us his righteousness in return. Amen.

FOR FURTHER REFLECTION, READ MATTHEW 27:15–26.

---

[15] Melanchthon, Philip. Commonplaces: Loci Communes 1521. St. Louis: Concordia Publishing House, 2014. 171

Jesus's Most Important Words

AND HE TOOK BREAD, AND WHEN HE HAD GIVEN THANKS, HE BROKE IT AND GAVE IT TO THEM, SAYING, "THIS IS MY BODY, WHICH IS GIVEN FOR YOU. DO THIS IN REMEMBRANCE OF ME." AND LIKEWISE THE CUP AFTER THEY HAD EATEN, SAYING, "THIS CUP THAT IS POURED OUT FOR YOU IS THE NEW COVENANT IN MY BLOOD."

Luke 22:19-20

For you. These are the two most important words Jesus ever spoke. Without them, Jesus's life, death, and resurrection mean nothing. Without these words, Jesus becomes another slogan-slinging teacher passing out pithy sayings and mantras to whisper to ourselves when life puts us in the fetal position. Without the words *for you*, the good news, the gospel, does not exist, only more rules.

Without these words, Christianity becomes meaningless. It becomes nothing more than a religious system for modifying behavior and moral improvement. It becomes no different than any other religion. Without the words *for you*, Christianity becomes another way in which God dispenses his wrath.

Many of Jesus's other words hold a familiar and popular place among people's hearts, but even these fall short without the words *for you*: "For God so loved the world" (John 3:16); "So whatever you wish that others would do to you, do also to them" (Matthew 7:12). Even the words "It is finished" (John 19:10) fall short on their own. In the context of the cross, we know what was finished, but who was it finished for? Did Jesus die for the Father, to save himself, or for the good, the morally upright, and the religiously righteous? No. Jesus died for you. It is finished for you.

The words *for you* are the most necessary words. Without them, we wouldn't know that Jesus's life, death, and resurrection apply to us. They would just be things that happened—maybe for someone out there. Without these words, we would have to earn our favor with God, our forgiveness, and our eternal life. Without them we have no hope, only despair.

But we have them. *We have these words that are the essence of the Gospel. Christ crucified for you. Christ died for you. Christ buried for you. Christ raised for you.*

Heavenly Father, you sent your Son, not for your own entertainment or out of boredom, but out of love and concern for us. Continue to remind us that the gospel of Christ crucified and Christ risen is for us. Amen.

FOR FURTHER REFLECTION, READ LUKE 22:14–20.

Answer Me

HEAR MY PRAYER, O LORD; GIVE EAR TO MY
PLEAS FOR MERCY! IN YOUR FAITHFULNESS
ANSWER ME, IN YOUR RIGHTEOUSNESS!

Psalm 143:1

The psalmist holds nothing back. *Answer me! Give ear to my pleas for mercy!* Does David know who he's speaking to? Does he not know the one to whom he prays created all things? Who does he think he is?

The question, however, is not who does David think he is, but who does David know his God to be? Such a tenacious prayer can only swell up from confidence in God's grace.

> **On this Good Friday, we marvel as Christ assumed our sin and died in our place. We behold the Lamb of God who took away the sin of the world. Today we hear the Lord's resounding, "Amen!" to the prayer of the psalmist as Christ declares from the cross, "It is finished" (John 19:30).**

The psalmist dares to pray with such boldness because of who his God is for him. His God will answer, not on account of David, but for the sake of the one who took David's place.

Today we pray with the psalmist, "Hear our prayer, give ear to our pleas for mercy, and in your faithfulness, in Christ our righteousness, answer us!" God has heard our pleas for mercy. As we meditate on the cross, we behold the answer to our prayers. We ponder our faithful Lord who answers us in this way: while we were still sinners, he gave his life unto death for us so we can be his own and live in his righteousness forever (Romans 5:8).

Heavenly Father, you made your Son who knew no sin to be our sin so we might become your righteousness. Comfort us through your gifts in word and sacrament as we meditate on the cross. Amen.

FOR FURTHER REFLECTION, READ ROMANS 8.

Exchanging Graves

NOW WHEN MARY CAME TO WHERE JESUS WAS AND SAW HIM, SHE FELL AT HIS FEET, SAYING TO HIM, "LORD, IF YOU HAD BEEN HERE, MY BROTHER WOULD NOT HAVE DIED."

John 11:32

Martha said them first (John 11:21), but Mary's words came with greater exasperation. Lord, you could have stopped this! Where were you? Martha's words took comfort in a future hope. Mary's words found sorrow in a hope lost. But Jesus's "late" arrival taught Mary and Martha (and teaches us too!) a greater truth about the Son of God. Jesus didn't come to prevent us from dying; he came to prevent us from staying dead.

Initially, Jesus appears to be all over the map in this story. He seemed content to stay where he was. In response to news of Lazarus's sickness, he said, "This illness does not lead to death" (John 11:4). Two days later he plainly stated, "Lazarus has died ... let us go to him" (11:14). What gives, Jesus? I thought you loved

Mary, Martha, and Lazarus? (11:5). Why did you say he wasn't going to die and then wait around till he did? By the time he arrived, "he found that Lazarus had already been in the tomb four days" (11:17).

In the midst of our sin and suffering, we can feel like Mary. We feel like God showed up too late to do anything. *Thanks for coming, God, but why didn't you prevent it from happening? Why didn't you stop me from that terrible sin? Where were you?* We feel let down, like God didn't keep his promise.

But like Lazarus, we're already dead in our trespasses and sins (Ephesians 2:1). By all appearances, our situation seems hopeless. The dead can't raise themselves. But Jesus had something bigger in mind by arriving "behind schedule." *He didn't arrive to merely call us out of the grave. He came to take our place in it.* To be our resurrection and life, Jesus had to die our death and rise our resurrection.

> **Jesus didn't come to prevent what already happened. He came to prevent what already happened from being permanent. Lazarus's death was not permanent. And because of Jesus, the Resurrection and the Life, neither is ours.**

Christ, Holy One of the Father, hold us fast in the resurrection you rose for us that first Easter Sunday. Amen.

FOR FURTHER REFLECTION, READ JOHN 11:1–44.

Do not be afraid,
for I know that you seek
Jesus who was crucified.
He is not here, for he has
risen, as he said.

MATTHEW 28:5-6

Made in the USA
Columbia, SC
02 January 2023